Your AV² Media Enhanced book gives you a fiction readalong online. Log on to www.av2books.com and enter the unique book code from this page to use your readalong.

AV² Readalong Navigation

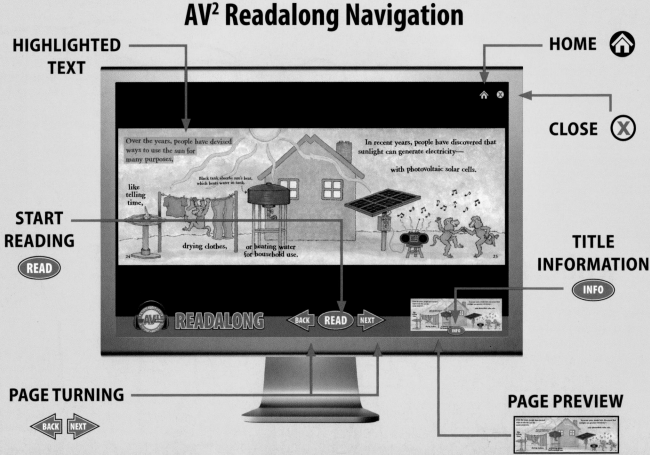

HIGHLIGHTED TEXT

HOME

CLOSE

START READING

TITLE INFORMATION

PAGE TURNING

PAGE PREVIEW

Go to **www.av2books.com**, and enter this book's unique code.

BOOK CODE

D 7 5 5 1 2 1

AV² by Weigl brings you media enhanced books that support active learning.

First Published by

ALBERT WHITMAN & COMPANY
Publishing children's books since 1919

Copyright©2013 AV² By Weigl. Library of Congress Cataloging-in-Publication Data is located on page 32.

THERE ARE TRILLIONS OF STARS IN THE UNIVERSE.
Our sun is one of them.

The sun looks bigger and brighter to us than other stars, because it's the closest star to Earth.

The sun is a huge, fiery gas ball.
It radiates, or sends, warmth and light
from 93,000,000 miles away.

More than a million Earths
could fit inside it!

Compared to the sun,
Earth would be about this size.

Plants and animals all over the world depend on the sun's energy to live.

Elephants certainly do. They need the sun to keep warm and to help grow the food they eat.

Elephants eat plants, and without the sun, plants can't live.

A male African elephant is Earth's biggest land animal. It can weigh as much as a truck. Trucks need lots of fuel. So do elephants.

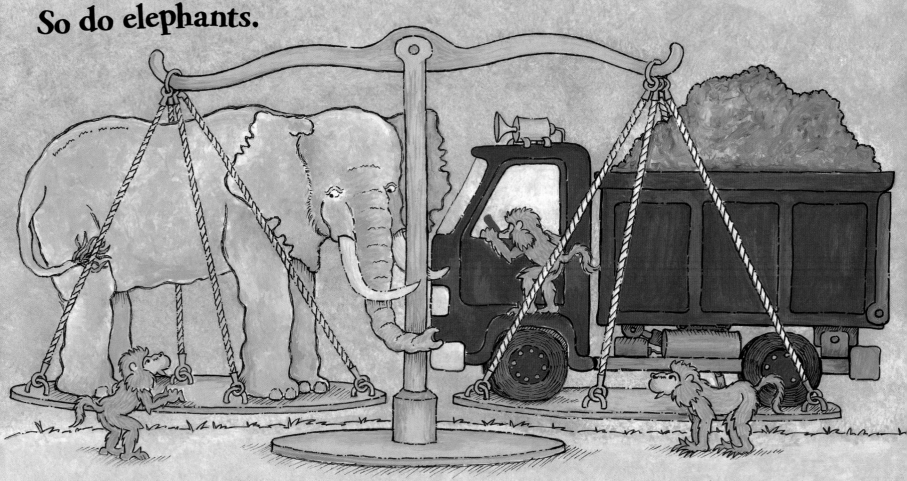

Some elephants eat 400 pounds of plants every day!

7

Plants need food, too. But with the help of the sun, plants can make their own food!

They do this by photosynthesis. It works like this: inside leaves is a green pigment called chlorophyll. Chlorophyll absorbs, or takes in, sunlight.

Carbon dioxide, a gas in the air, enters through the leaves . . .

and water is drawn from the ground by the plant's roots.

Chlorophyll, using the sun's energy, helps transform the water and carbon dioxide into a sugar called glucose—the food plants need to live and grow.

In photosynthesis, the water inside plants splits into its two parts, oxygen and hydrogen.

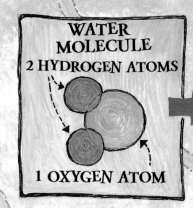

WATER MOLECULE
2 HYDROGEN ATOMS

1 OXYGEN ATOM

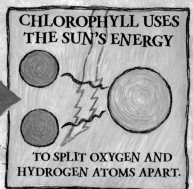

CHLOROPHYLL USES THE SUN'S ENERGY

TO SPLIT OXYGEN AND HYDROGEN ATOMS APART.

The oxygen part is not needed. It is released into the air,

and animals and people breathe it.

Then they breathe out carbon dioxide— and plants use it to make more glucose.

When people and animals eat plants, they use the glucose for their own energy.

Plants and animals are truly life partners— helped along by the sun!

Animals need to drink water, just as plants do. Especially elephants.

A thirsty elephant may drink 50 gallons a day!

The hot sun can dry up a water hole . . .

and help fill it up again! How?

The sun's heat evaporates ocean water,

turning it into water vapor.

The water vapor rises and forms clouds,

leaving the salt behind.

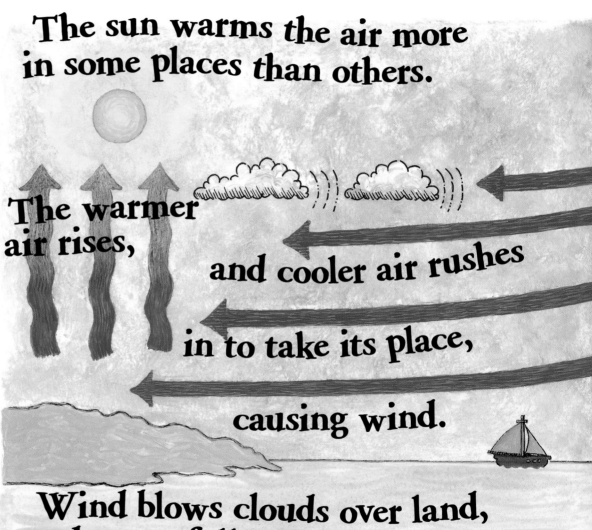

The sun warms the air more in some places than others.

The warmer air rises,

and cooler air rushes

in to take its place,

causing wind.

Wind blows clouds over land, and water falls as rain or snow.

13

Some of the rain will fall on grassy savannas where elephants live,

and some will flow into the water holes where elephants drink.

Water will soak into the
ground and help plants grow,
so elephants can eat.

15

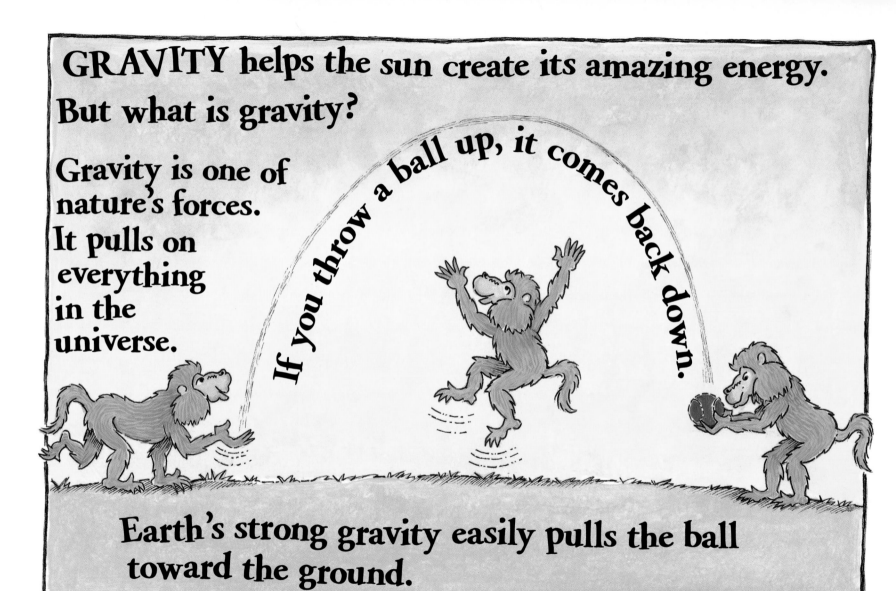

GRAVITY helps the sun create its amazing energy. But what is gravity?

Gravity is one of nature's forces. It pulls on everything in the universe.

If you throw a ball up, it comes back down.

Earth's strong gravity easily pulls the ball toward the ground.

The more material, or mass, an object has, the more gravity pulls on it.

That's why an elephant weighs so much more than a baboon.

Earth's gravity pulls on the elephant with much more force.

The sun's gravity is much, much stronger than Earth's, because the sun has much greater mass.

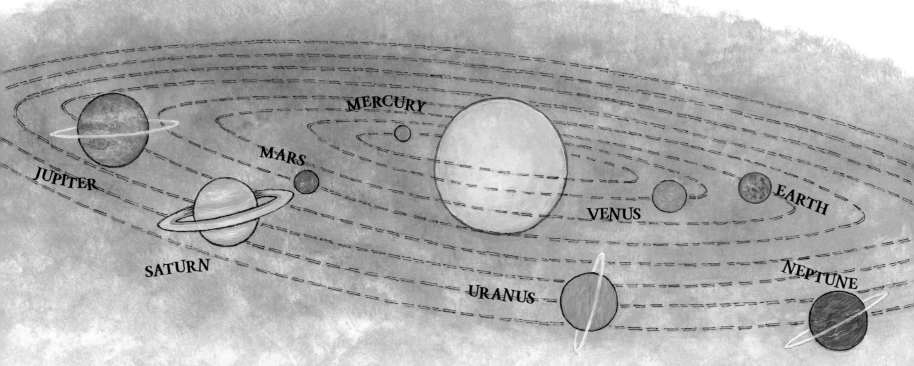

The sun's powerful gravity holds all 8 planets in their orbits, keeping them from flying off into the cold darkness of space!

How does gravity help the sun generate energy?

The sun is not solid, like Earth. It's made up mostly of hydrogen gas.

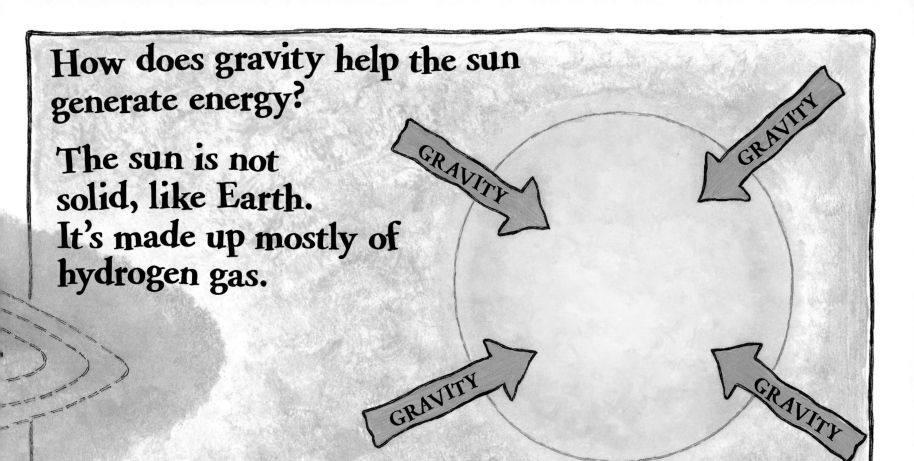

Gravity pushes on the sun's surface and compresses the hydrogen gas inside, causing the hydrogen atoms to heat up.

At the center, or core, of the sun, the pressure is so great that the hydrogen atoms are transformed into helium atoms.

This process, called nuclear fusion, generates great amounts of heat and light.

Nuclear fusion heats the sun's core to an amazing 28,000,000 degrees F., or 15,500,000 degrees C.

CORE

This tremendous heat slowly travels through a gas layer called the radiative zone,

RADIATIVE ZONE

then through a layer called the convective zone, which transfers heat to the sun's surface, or photosphere.

CONVECTIVE ZONE

PHOTOSPHERE

By the time the heat reaches the photosphere, it has cooled to about 10,000 degrees F., or 5,500 degrees C.—much cooler than at the core, but still 30 times hotter than an oven baking a cake!

The corona is a very thin gas that makes up most of the sun's atmosphere. It can be seen as a bright cloudy halo around the darkened sun during a total solar eclipse.

SOLAR ECLIPSE

A total solar eclipse occurs when the moon passes between the Earth and sun, blocking out the sun's light.

Moon moving in front of the sun

Total solar eclipse

Moon moving away from sun

Just above the sun's surface, a lower layer of atmospheric gas called the chromosphere transfers the sun's heat to the corona—heating the corona to more than 3,000,000 degrees F., or 1,700,000 degrees C.

CORONA

The corona reaches out hundreds of thousands of miles and radiates the sun's heat and light into space—

sending some of its life-giving energy all the way to Earth!

Over the years, people have devised ways to use the sun for many purposes,

like telling time,

Black tank absorbs sun's heat, which heats water in tank.

drying clothes,

or heating water for household use.

In recent years, people have discovered that sunlight can generate electricity—

with photovoltaic solar cells.

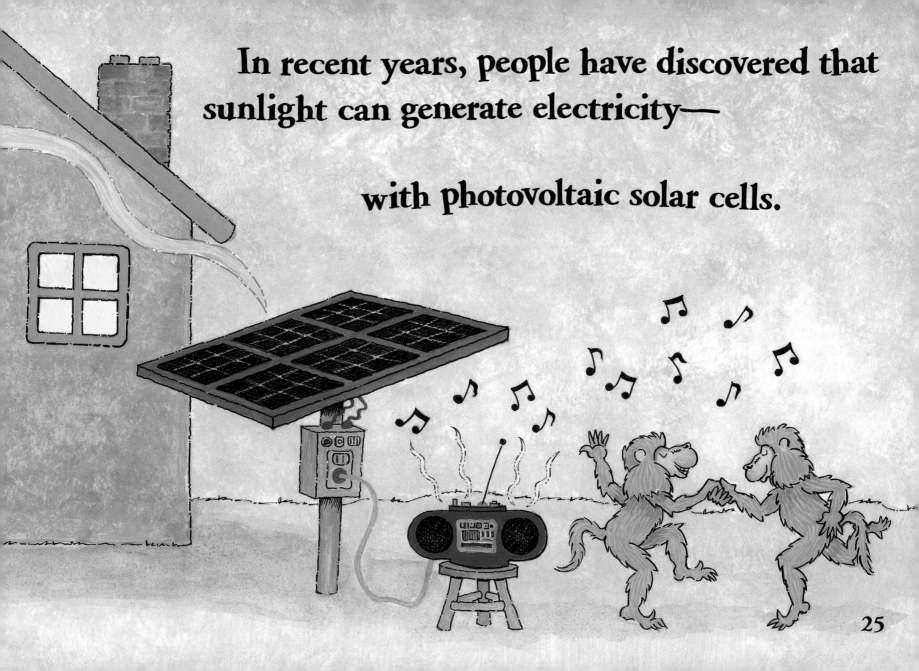

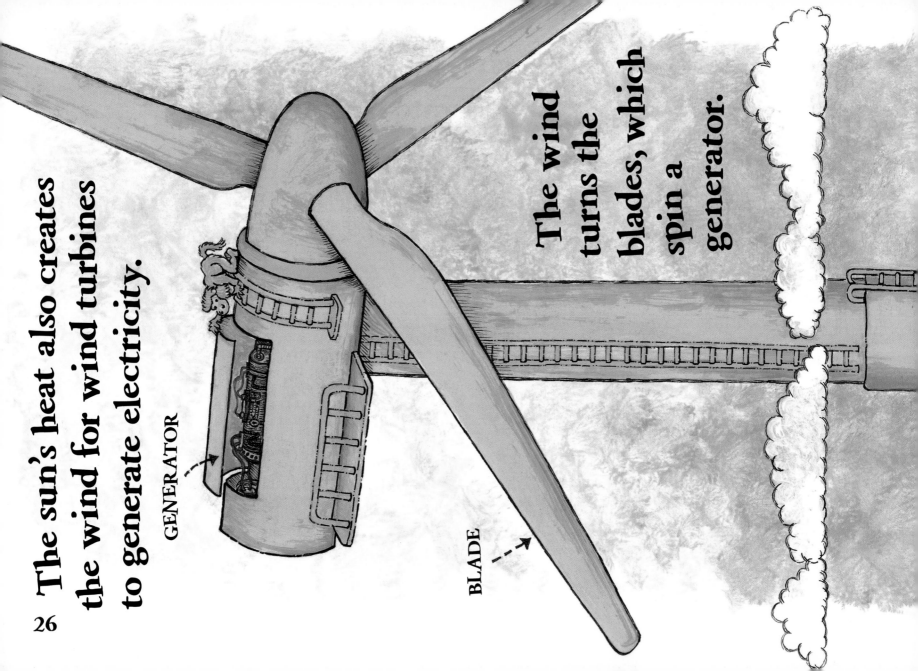

The sun's heat also creates the wind for wind turbines to generate electricity.

GENERATOR

The wind turns the blades, which spin a generator.

BLADE

26

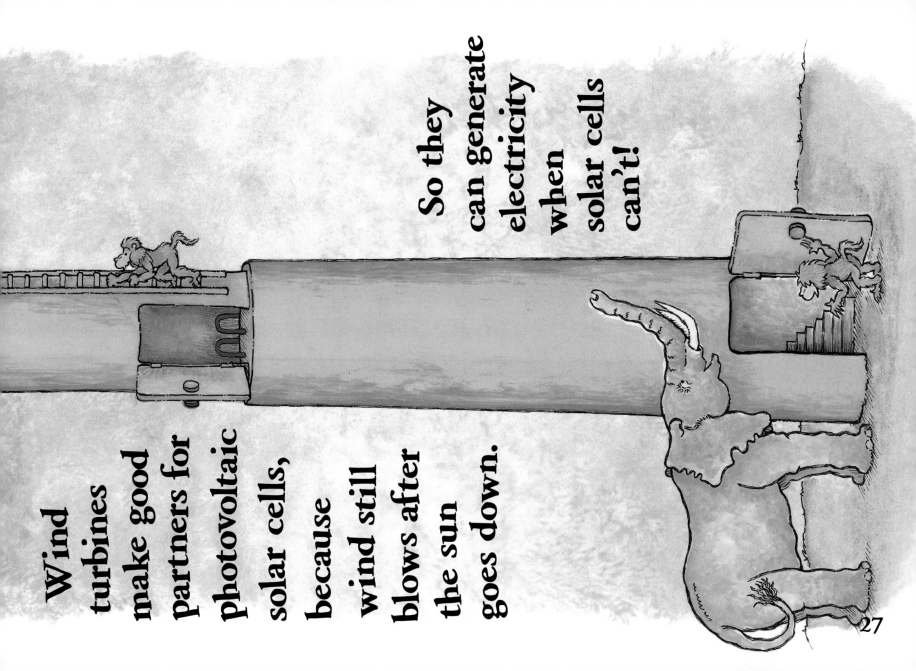

Wind turbines make good partners for photovoltaic solar cells, because wind still blows after the sun goes down.

So they can generate electricity when solar cells can't!

27

When we look up at the night sky, we can see some of the trillions of stars in the universe.

No one could ever count them all.

But not one of them is as important
to us as our very own star,
the sun!

DID YOU KNOW?

1. The sun began to form about 4.6 billion years ago

from a giant cloud of space dust.

2. 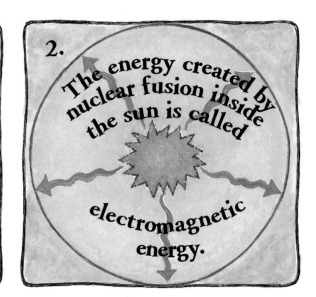 The energy created by nuclear fusion inside the sun is called electromagnetic energy.

3. Sunspots are darker areas on the sun's surface 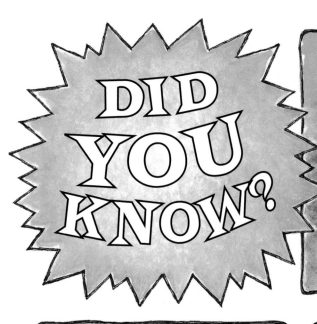 that are a little cooler than the surface.

4. If you could drive from Earth to the sun, traveling at 60 miles per hour, it would take about 175 years . . .

5.  but it takes sunlight only 8.3 minutes to travel the same distance!

6. The sun contains about 99%

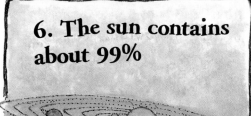

of all the mass in the solar system.

7. 5 million tons of the sun's mass

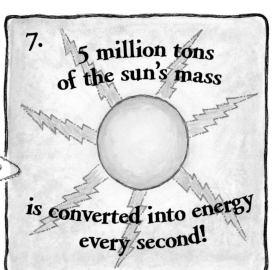

is converted into energy every second!

8. Only a small fraction of the sun's energy—

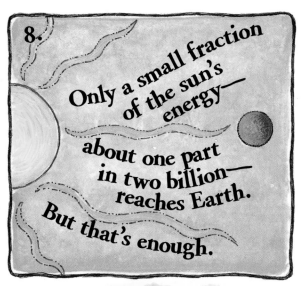

about one part in two billion— reaches Earth. But that's enough.

9. Huge flares of hot gases called prominences

shoot out from the sun's surface thousands of miles into the corona.

10. Never look directly at the sun— it can damage your eyes.

And too much sun can burn your skin.

Someday, the sun will use up all its fuel and stop shining . . .

but don't worry— it won't happen for about 5 billion years!

A THANK YOU NOTE TO THE WORLD'S SCIENTISTS

Ancient people knew the sun was important. It measured out their days as it moved across the sky. It kept them warm and gave them light. They knew that when the sun set at the end of each day and the sky turned dark, they'd better return to their caves to avoid the danger of wild animals and to sleep until the sun returned.

Yes, our ancestors knew very well the sun was important. But until the advent of scientific inquiry, and especially the invention of scientific tools such as microscopes and telescopes, people did not know what the sun was made of or how it worked.

Without astronomers, the scientists who study planets and stars, we wouldn't know that the sun was the center of the solar system, or how gravity controls the orbits of planets. Without physicists, the scientists who study physical matter, we'd never have learned what kind of energy radiates from the sun, or how its core creates energy from nuclear fusion.

The study of biology and physics together has revealed to us the miracle of photosynthesis, and climate scientists have learned over the years how the sun's heat is the energy behind all the world's weather systems.

The tireless and dedicated work of scientists in many different fields, from the middle ages through modern times, has continued to add to the world's knowledge about our sun. New information is being discovered every year.

Thank you, scientists, throughout history and around the world, for studying the sun and revealing all the things it does for us on Earth. Without your work, a book such as this would not be possible.

Published by AV² by Weigl
350 5th Avenue, 59th Floor New York, NY 10118
Copyright ©2013 AV² by Weigl
Printed in the United States of America in North Mankato, Minnesota
1 2 3 4 5 6 7 8 9 0 16 15 14 13 12
Text and illustrations copyright © 2010 by Robert E. Wells.
Published in 2010 by Albert Whitman & Company.

052012
WEP160512

Library of Congress Cataloging-in-Publication Data
Wells, Robert E.
Why do elephants need the sun? / by Robert E. Wells.
    p. cm.
ISBN 978-1-61913-142-2 (hard cover : alk. paper)
1. Sun--Juvenile literature. 2. Sunshine--Juvenile literature. 3. Water cycle--Juvenile literature. 4. Photosynthesis--Juvenile literature. I. Title.
QB521.5.W448 2013
523.7--dc23   2012018611